Basic Budgeting:
The Simple Way for Anyone and Everyone to be in Control of Their Finances

Randi Lynn Millward

I0159841

Advance Praise for
Basic Budgeting:
The Simple Way for Anyone and Everyone to be in Control of Their Finances

"Randi Millward's new book, *Basic Budgeting: The Simple Way for Anyone and Everyone to be in Control of Their Finances*, really does make the budgeting process easy. While to many people today, budget is a four-letter word, Randi does a great job of helping people to know the importance of having a money-spending plan. She provides sample forms and categories that add to the totality and accuracy of the process. The painless methods set forth makes a person not only feel better about the process, but actually helps a person to look past the "budget" to the results of being in control. This is a must-read book for any person struggling with their finances because since it is so straightforward, 'anyone' can do it."

- Bob Marette
Author of *"From A Millstone To A Milestone: Get Out of Debt in 5-7 Years, Including Mortgage by Applying God's Principles"* and
"SCRIPTURAL CALENDAR: A Daily Guide To Help You Hide God's Word In Your Heart."

"Randi Lynn Millward has a wonderfully concise, easy to understand way to provide practical advice on how to control personal finances.
Through her weekly column hosted on *SingleMom.com*, Randi uses her financial skills to advise the large community of single moms on day to day budget management issues.
We are grateful for her contribution."

- SingleMom.com

"As it has been said within my faith by President Heber J. Grant: 'If there is any one thing that will bring peace and contentment into the human heart, and into the family, it is to live within our means.'
So true, no matter what stage of life you are in: rich, poor, middle class, single or married, a budget will help you have a financial plan. You will be able to live within your means while preparing for future events such as vacations, college, wedding, and most importantly unexpected emergencies.
My husband and I will budget our whole lives through, whether we make $20,000 a year or $200,000 a year. This book explains simply why you would want to do so."

- Julie Thompson
www.mylilbudgetbook.etsy.com

Basic Budgeting:

The Simple Way for Anyone and Everyone to be in Control of Their Finances

Randi Lynn Millward

Disclaimer: This book is designed to provide ideas and information about budgeting. Every effort has been made to make it as complete and accurate as possible, but no warranty or fitness is implied or included.

This book and its contents are not legal advice. If you desire legal counsel, consult a lawyer. For professional financial advice, consult a licensed professional.

No profit, warranty, or fitness is guaranteed from using any of the information herein.

It is the sole responsibility of the reader to seek professional financial expertise with regard to his or her own personal finances when necessary.

The author and publisher are not liable for any loss or damages sustained by, or resulting from, any information contained in this book.

ISBN 10: 0-9827334-0-2
ISBN 13: 9780982733400

Thanks & Dedication

To God, to my family, and to all of the people who are wondering where their money went.

Basic Budgeting:

The Simple Way for Anyone and Everyone to be in Control of Their Finances

Table of Contents

Introduction

By choosing to read this book, you've taken the first step toward being in control of your finances. After all, that is the goal of budgeting.

Whether you want to get out of debt, live within your means, or just know where your money is going, a budget is a great first step!

~ ~ ~ ~ ~ ~ ~

My Experience with Budgeting

My family has been on a budget for years now. At first it was difficult, but now it comes as second nature to us.

We're a family of five. I'm a stay-at-home mom. My husband works full-time. We're not rich, but we're not poor either. You don't have to be either rich or poor to have a budget though. Anyone with an income can have a budget.

Before we had children, my husband and I both worked. After he got out of the military, he wanted to have a baby right away. He was a laborer. I worked in restaurants and did some private housekeeping. Although I wanted children, I wanted to wait until we could afford for me to stay home with them.

My husband got a better job. I slowed down to one restaurant job and only a couple private housekeeping jobs. We were only two people, our bills were reasonable, but we couldn't figure out where our money was going. I was beginning to think that I'd never be able to be a stay-at-home mom.

After feeling broke for so long, I finally gave in to the idea of a budget. We were young. I thought budgeting was just something older people did, but for lack of a better idea, I decided to give it a try.

My husband wasn't exactly on-board with it at first. He thought it would be too much work. But he agreed to try it.

For one month, we didn't spend any differently. We just recorded all of our expenditures, in our pre-determined categories. When we totaled our expenditures, we were amazed. Now we knew where our money was going, and it was clear that we needed to control our spending.

The next month, we started trying to live on a budget. However, we cheated. When we ran out of money in a certain category, we just spent money from our savings account. We did that for months, until we were down to about $37 left in savings.

Then, it was time to face reality. The only way we could possibly be in control of our finances was if we made a budget and actually followed it.

We made a new budget. We adjusted it monthly as needed. It took us about a year to finally be able to consistently follow our budget. Then, we decided to try for a baby.

I planned on staying at home with the baby once she was born, but I was a waitress, so I was really looking forward to getting "pregnancy tips". I was going to save my tips to buy all of the baby gear - the crib, stroller, baby monitors, etc.

I quit housekeeping, but I planned to continue waitressing until the baby was born. In my second month though, I ran into some complications. At first, the doctor told me to take two weeks off, and I did, but the problem didn't resolve itself as expected. He told me that we'd have to take it week by week to see when or if I'd be able to return to work, but I ended up having to just leave my job.

Then, we were living on one income - earlier than planned, whether we liked it or not. Like everyone else though, we did what we had to do, and we made it work. I doubt we could have without having a budget. We cut back a bit, but our budget let us see where our money was going. We adjusted our budget and still had the security of knowing that we'd be able to cover our bills. It was comforting to know that.

Now, over three years later, we have three children - and one budget - and it works great for us! We're well on our way to accomplishing our financial goals of paying off our mortgage early and saving and investing for retirement.

What & Why

Many people don't know what a budget is, what a budget isn't, and why to bother even having a budget. Most people that I've encountered believe the myths that a budget is a financial diet, that it means that you can't spend money, or that the goal of having a budget is to spend as little money as possible. All of those myths make budgeting sound quite unappealing, if not completely impossible. After all, most diets involving food fail. Why would the outcome of financial dieting be any different?

A budget is not the same as a diet. Your goal is not to spend as little as possible, unless you want it to be. Budgeting is simply organizing your expenses and allocating funds. It's deciding what to spend your money on and how much money to spend on those things. Budgeting is controlling your finances, knowing where your money is going, and knowing how much of that money is going to the things you're spending it on.

Too many people wonder where their money has gone. At the end of the month, although they've received two paychecks that month, they don't have the money to pay their electric bill. They know they earn enough money to cover their bills, but they're not sure where the money has gone and why they can't afford to pay their bills. If they had a budget, they'd know where their money had gone. If they followed a budget, their money would be exactly where it was supposed to be - in their checking account, waiting to be handed over to the electric company!

Since budgeting is just deciding what you're going to spend your money on, you can include anything you want, and can afford, in your budget. You don't have to sacrifice the things you enjoy. If you frequently play golf, you can allot a certain amount of money to be spent on golf. If you like to go out to eat, you can allot money for that.

You don't have to give up the things you enjoy. By budgeting, you decide beforehand that you're going to spend money on those things. You also decide how much money you're going to spend on those things.

With a budget, you're in control of your finances. You decide what you're going to spend your money on. You decide how much money you're going to spend on those things. Then, you spend no more than the allotted amount on the things on which you've chosen to spend your money.

Having a budget puts you in control of your finances. It shows you where your money is going. It gives you the peace of mind of knowing that you'll be able to pay your bills. It answers the question of whether or not you're able to afford a purchase.

If you'd like, your budget could help you save money. By being aware of your expenditures, you could review your purchases and identify any unnecessary expenses. Once you get good at following a budget, which could take many months, you could begin to slowly reduce the money you allot to various categories. You could slowly reduce the money allotted to take-out or movies a few dollars each month until you're at your target amount. It won't happen overnight, but by being more aware of your purchases, you become more purposeful about your spending.

If you're feeling restricted by the amount of money you allotted to a certain category, you may resort to more creative ways to stretch your dollar (coupons, sales, online discount codes, etc.), or you may just allot more money to that category next month. After all, your monthly budget isn't set in stone. You can adjust it monthly until you find the distribution of expenditures that works for you.

For example, toward the end of summer, you may allot more money to the clothing category, knowing that you'll be buying your children new school clothes. To make up for that, you could subtract some money from your grocery category, knowing that your children will be eating their lunches at school rather than at home.

When you're on a budget, it doesn't mean that you're poor. It means that you're taking control of your finances. You decide how much to spend and what to spend it on. Then, you adjust your budget monthly, if necessary, to make it fit your lifestyle.

With a budget, you're controlling your finances, your finances aren't controlling you. You don't have to be rich to have a budget. You don't have to be poor to have a budget. You just have to have an income.

For a budget to work, the amount of income you have doesn't matter. All that matters is how you spend it.

Tracking your expenditures without staying within the boundaries you set is merely keeping a record of your finances. Being in control of your finances by staying within the boundaries you set is budgeting.

Money Managing Methods

When being on a budget, there are various methods you could use to control your finances. You'll be deciding beforehand the amount of money you'll be spending in each of your budget categories, but you'll need to find a way to stay within those allotments.

The Envelope Method

Perhaps the simplest method is the "envelope method". When using the envelope method, you'll use envelopes as your bank. You'll have an envelope for each of your budget categories. You'll write the name of the category on the envelope, along with the amount of money allotted to the category. Then, at the beginning of every month, you'll put the allotted monetary amounts of cash in each envelope and spend only the money in the envelope for the allotted purchases that month. When the cash is gone, you quit spending.

If you allot $500 for groceries, you write "Groceries - $500" on an envelope. Then, you put

$500 cash in the envelope at the beginning of the month. Throughout the month, when you need groceries, you take money out of the envelope, buy groceries, and put any unspent money back in the envelope. You only spend what's in the envelope, no more than that. When the cash is gone, since you can't spend what you don't have, you don't spend any more money.

The envelope method may be difficult to follow, with empty envelopes sometimes seeming to pop up on you, but it also requires less time than writing down all of your purchases to keep track of your remaining balances in your budget categories. To make the envelope method a little easier, you could recount the money whenever you spend some and write the remaining balances on the backs of the envelopes. That'll help you be more aware of the amount of money you have left to spend without taking too much time or effort.

The Complete Written Record Method

With the "complete written record method" of budgeting, you record all of your expenditures in the appropriate categories and subtract the expenditures from the allotment to get your new remaining balance.

For example, when you buy groceries, in the grocery category of your budget you write "2 gallons milk, 3 lbs. chicken, 2 frozen pizzas, 3 containers yogurt, 2 bags frozen peas, 4 boxes cereal - $46.24". If you had $600 in the grocery category, you subtract $46.24 from $600, leaving you with your new balance of $553.76. The next time you buy groceries, you write down the items you bought and the amount you spent. Then, you subtract the amount you spend from your previous balance of $553.76. You continue doing that until either you're at a zero balance, or the month is over.

The complete written record method of budgeting is the most tedious and time-consuming, but it is also the best method to make you truly aware of where your money is going. If you're content with your spending, you can just leave your budget as it is. If you'd like to cut back on your spending a bit, by using the complete written record method, you can see what exactly you're spending too much money on. For example, if you review your budget and notice that you're buying alot of tv dinners, you could try to make more homemade meals to save some money in the grocery category.

The complete written record method of budgeting can show you exactly where your money is going. It can help you recognize unnecessary expenditures. It can also help you stay within your budget by allowing you to check the remaining allotment of any category in your budget at any time by just glancing at the balance.

The Minimal Written Record Method
With the "minimal written record method" of budgeting, you keep a written record of the amounts of your expenditures. You write down the amount of the expenditure in the appropriate category, but you don't write down what you spend the money on. Then, you subtract the expenditures from the allotment to get your new remaining balance.

For example, if you go grocery shopping and buy 2 gallons of milk, 3 pounds of chicken, 2 frozen pizzas, 3 containers of yogurt, 2 bags of frozen peas, and 4 boxes of cereal for a total of $46.24, all you write down in the grocery category of your budget is "46.24". If you had $600 in the grocery category, you subtract $46.24 from $600, leaving you with your new balance of $553.76. The next time you buy groceries, you subtract the amount you spend from your previous balance of $553.76. Each time you spend money, you subtract it from your remaining balance and get your new allotment for the remainder of the month. You continue doing that until either you're at a zero balance, or the month is over.

The minimal written record method of budgeting may be the most convenient option for people who prefer credit and/or debit cards over cash. It's also good for people who cringe at the idea of writing down every individual item that they spend money on. With the minimal written record method, you're still able to check the remaining allotment of any category in your budget at any time by just glancing at the balance.

The Combination Cash & Written Record Method

The "combination cash & written record method" of budgeting combines the envelope method and the written record method. With the combination cash & written record method of budgeting, part of your allotted money is in the form of cash. The other part can be spent by debit or credit card.

When using this method, you deduct the amount of cash you're putting in an envelope from the amount allotted in the category. You don't keep a record of the cash you spend, though you may note the expenditures on the envelope to keep track of the cash balance if you'd like, but you do keep a written record of non-cash expenditures.

For example, if you allot $600 to the grocery category, and you want $200 of it to be in cash, in the grocery category of your budget, you write "envelope cash - $200". Then, you subtract the $200 from the $600 and are left with a $400 balance for non-cash grocery expenditures and $200 for grocery expenditures paid in cash. When you spend the cash, you don't write the purchases in the grocery category because the cash has already been accounted for when you wrote "cash - $200". When you pay for groceries with your credit or debit card, you record those expenditures in the grocery category because they're non-cash purchases.

The combination cash & written record method of budgeting may be the most flexible method of managing your expenditures. It's beneficial if you shop at stores that don't take credit cards or if you frequently make small purchases that you don't want to bother complicating your bank statement with by using your debit card. It's also a beneficial method of budgeting when one family member prefers to spend cash and another prefers to use debit or credit cards.

Deciding on Categories

When beginning a budget, one of the first things you need to do is establish your budget categories. For example, will you have a single "food" category, or will you divide it into "groceries" and "takeout"? Will you have just an "entertainment" category, or will you have "golf" and "bowling" categories?

Bills

To establish your budget categories, begin with your bills. The bills category will then be subdivided to include all of your monthly bills. It will include your mortgage, vehicle payments, vehicle insurance, life insurance, electricity, gas heat, garbage, cable, water, sewage, telephone, cell phone, internet, and any other bill that you pay regularly. Even if it's a bill that you only pay every other month, every quarter, or even just yearly, include it - a bill is a bill.

To handle your irregular bills (bi-monthly, yearly, quarterly, etc.) add up the entire amount that you pay per year, and divide it by 12. That will tell you how much money you need to allot every month, to be put in a separate account until the bill becomes due, to easily cover the cost of the bill without wrecking your budget with an occasional large expenditure.

See the example below.

Bills

Electric	$70
Vehicle Insurance	($300 quarterly) $100 to alternate account
Life Insurance	($120 yearly) $10 to alternate account
Telephone	$40
Garbage	$35

Once you've figured out your expenses for each of your bills, add them up to find out the total amount of money you need per month to pay your bills. That figure will help you determine how much you can afford to spend on your other expenses. I'll go into greater detail about this in a later chapter.

Other Categories
Your other categories are for the things that you spend money on that aren't bills. They include, but are not limited to, things like food, diapers, cleaning supplies, movie rentals, gas for your vehicles, gifts, and other miscellaneous items.

You could make a few broad categories or many very specific categories for those expenditures. For example, you could lump groceries and takeout into a single "food" category, or you could keep them as two separate categories. The choice is yours. A couple examples are listed below.

Categories:
1. Food
2. Entertainment
3. Household Expenditures

or

Categories:
1. Groceries
2. Takeout
3. Golf
4. Movies
5. Diapers
6. Cleaning Supplies

Once you've decided on your categories, make sure you and anyone else in your household who helps out with purchases knows exactly which items go in which categories. If you go to the movies and buy popcorn, do you put the entire amount spend in the entertainment category, or do you put the cost of the movie tickets in the entertainment category and the cost of the popcorn in the food category?

The choice is yours, but you still need to make sure everyone in your household follows the decision. If they don't, you could end up without enough money in one category and too much money in another. You could re-adjust your budget monthly to make up for those fluctuations, but it would be easier to make a decision about your categories and be consistent with it.

After some practice, it will get easier. You can add new categories or consolidate existing ones. Just set up some basic categories to get you started, and adjust them according to your needs as often as necessary.

Tracking Your Expenses

       Before actually beginning a budget, you'll need to have an idea of your expenditures. How much money will you allot to household items? What amount will you allot to food?

       You could just guess on these figures, but in doing that, you could just be setting yourself up for failure. If you don't know how much you normally spend, the amount you allot may prove too restrictive for you to stay within.

       You need to make your budget realistic. If you spend $700 per month on food, but you only allot $400 because you're unaware of how much you usually spend, you can't expect to keep your grocery expenditures within the boundary of $400. You would have to slash your spending almost in half, and even if you were able to do that one month, you'd probably eventually end up feeling too restricted and quit budgeting altogether.

       In order to be realistic with your budgeting, you need to know the actual amount of your monthly expenditures. To learn the actual amount, you'll need to track all of your expenditures for at least one month before beginning a budget. Spend as you normally would, but record your purchases.

You've probably already decided on your budget categories. Now you'll use them to track your expenses. While you're tracking your expenses, don't allot money to the budget categories because you're not yet budgeting. All you're doing is tracking your expenditures.

When you spend money, write it down in the appropriate category. You can keep detailed records, simple records, or a combination of the two. Just make sure you right down the monetary amounts.

Do that for at least an entire month, though you could do it for two or three months if you'd like. At the end of the month, add up the expenses in each category.

If you recorded your expenditures for two months, add up the amount in each category for the two months, and divide by two to get the average monthly amount you spend in each category. If you recorded your expenditures for three months, add up the amount in each category for the three months, and divide by three to get the average monthly amount you spend in each category.

Once you know your average expenditures, you can budget those amounts in your upcoming monthly budget, you can round the numbers up or down, or you could try to cut back by budgeting a slightly lower amount.

See the following examples.

Tracking Your Expenditures
(Using combination detailed and simple records)

Food - June

milk, eggs, bread, yogurt	$14
groceries at the corner market	$56
takeout	$34
groceries	$279
pizza	$28
groceries	$228

Total Spent on Food in June: $639

Food - July

5 school fundraiser pizzas	$75
groceries	$323
takeout	$32
groceries	$198
groceries	$82
fast food burgers & milkshakes	$28

Total Spent on Food in July: $738

Food - August

groceries	$402
farmer's market corn	$18
church bake sale pie	$8
groceries	$76
chicken, bread, oranges	$13
groceries	$41

Total Spent on Food in August: $ 558

Averaging Your Expenditures

June Food: $639
July Food: $738
August Food: $558

June + July + August = three-month total
$639 + $738 + $558 = $1935

total divided by number of months = average monthly
expenditure amount
$1935/3 = $645

According to those figures, based on the records in the previous example, $645 would be the average monthly grocery expenditure amount.

Once you have your average for each budget category, you can decide how much money to allot to each category to begin your budget with. If you're content with those numbers, great. If you want to try to cut back in some categories, budget an amount slightly lower than your average. Keep budgeting slightly less each month until you reach your goal.

Your Real Monthly Income

At first, it may sound odd that you have to figure out what your monthly income is, but it could be different from what you might expect it to be. You may earn an hourly rate, be paid a fixed salary, or earn commission only. You may earn the same amount every month, or your income may fluctuate. Even if you know your gross income, you may not be aware of your net income.

If you're going to allot the same amount of money for expenditures every month, you'll need to know your average monthly income. Since not every month has the same number of days, your income may vary from month to month. If you only use a month with 31 days to figure out your income, you may budget more than you earn in months with fewer days. In order for you to establish a budget, you'll need to know your average monthly income so that, at the end of the year, the total of your monthly expenditures doesn't exceed your yearly income.

To budget using your average monthly income, if you earn more money than you budgeted in a certain month, transfer it to a savings account. That way, if you earn less money than you budgeted in a shorter month, you will still have the money to spend, as long as you've correctly calculated your yearly income and you stay within your budget. Just take it from the savings account that you're using to hold your excess monthly income.

To begin figuring out your monthly income, you'll want to look at one of your pay stubs. Your net income is the amount you earn after deductions. Deductions may include taxes, union dues, insurance, mandatory retirement contributions, and other expenses deducted directly from your paycheck.

Net Income for Hourly Rate Pay

As an example, if you earn $10 per hour, 8 hours per day, 5 days per week, for 2 weeks (the average pay period), your gross income would be $800 per pay period. However, your paycheck probably isn't in the amount of $800. Your paycheck, the amount of money you actually have to budget, may only be $685. So, your net income is $685 per paycheck.

Instead of earning $10 per hour, you're actually only netting $8.50 per hour, or 85% of your hourly rate.

You can use the following formula to figure out your hourly net income.

hourly rate x hours worked = gross pay
net pay/gross pay = hourly net income

Example:
$10 x 80 = $800
$685/$800 = 0.85 or 85%

Net Income for Salary Pay

Figuring out your net income if you're paid by salary is pretty much the same as figuring out your hourly net income.

If your gross monthly salary is $2,500, your monthly paycheck will, of course, be in an amount less than $2,500. As an example, your monthly paycheck may be $1,750. To figure out your monthly net income, use the following formula.

monthly net pay/monthly gross pay = monthly net income

Example:
$1,750/$2,500 = 0.7 or 70%

If you only know your gross annual salary, you'll need to divide it by 12 to get your gross monthly salary. As an example, if your gross annual salary is $30,000, you divide it by the number of months in a year to get your gross monthly income of $2,500.

To figure out your monthly net income, use the following formula.

annual salary/12 = gross monthly income
net pay/gross pay = net income

Example:
$30,000/12 = $2,500
$2,500/$1,750 = 0.7 or 70%

Net Income for Commission Only Pay

If you work for commission only, you'll need to use your pay from the previous year, or an average of multiple previous years, to figure out your average income. Since your income could vary greatly from month to month, you'll need to figure out your average yearly income and divide it by 12.

If, for example, you earned $60,000 last year, $55,000 the previous year, and $59,000 the year before that, your average yearly income for the previous three years would be $58,000.

If that was your gross income, and your deductions were 15% of your pay, your actual average yearly income would be $49,300.

If $58,000 was your net income, then $58,000 would be your actual average yearly income from the past three years.

To figure out your average yearly income, see the example below.

Year 1 Income: $60,000
Year 2 Income: $55,000
Year 3 Income: $59,000

$60,000+$55,000+$59,000 = $174,000

$174,000/3 = $58,000

If $58,000 was your average yearly net income, and your deductions were 15% of your pay, your actual average yearly net income would be $49,300.

$58,000 x 0.15 = $8,700
$58,000 - $8,700 = $49,300

If your average yearly net income was $58,000, your actual average monthly income, the monthly amount that you would budget for expenditures, would be $4,833. ($4,833.33333 rounded to $4,833)

$58,000/12 = $4,833.33333
$4,833.33333 rounded to the nearest dollar is $4,833

If your average yearly net income was $49,300, your actual average monthly income, the monthly amount that you would budget for expenditures, would be $4,108. ($4,108.33333 rounded to $4,108)

$49,300/12 = $4,108.33333
$4,108.33333 rounded to the nearest dollar is $4,108.

Tithes

If you tithe 10% of your income, don't forget to deduct your tithe when calculating your income. If, for example, your gross yearly income is $40,000, you'd deduct $4,000 to get $36,000. Then, you'd figure in your deductions to get your average actual yearly income.

See the example below.

Gross Income: $40,000
$40,000 x 10% = $4,000
$40,000 - $4,000 = $36,000
Deductions: 20%
$40,000 x 20% = $8,000
$40,000 - $4,000 - $8,000 = $28,000
Actual Average Yearly Income = $28,000

41

Setting Up Your Budget

Using the previous chapters, you've figured out your income and expenditures. You've figured out your bills and your other expenditure categories. Now it's time to put all of that information together to create your own monthly budget.

Begin with your income amount. Write it at the top of a sheet of paper. Below your income, write down your bills. Below your bills, write down your other expenditure categories. Subtract the amount of your bills from your income to get the amount of money you have left to spend in your other expenditure categories. With that figure, and with the records of your expenditures in each of the categories, allot the appropriate amount of money to each of the categories, subtracting that amount from the remaining balance available to spend, until you reach $0. Re-adjust the amounts if you come up short. Just make sure that your expenditures match your income.

If you're used to spending more than you earn, it may take you a while to allot money to your categories without exceeding your income. Take as long as you need and re-adjust as many times as necessary.

You can create your budget any time of the month. Just make sure it's ready by the beginning of the month in which you'll be using it.

The following chapter contains sample budgets that may be of help to you.

Sample Budgets
&
Budget Pages

Sample Budget #1

Income: $2,000
Bills: $ 1,200
Other Expenditures: $800
>   Food: $400
>   Household Expenditures: $80
>   Gas for Vehicles: $50
>   Diapers: $100
>   College Savings Plan: $50
>   Bowling: $75
>   Miscellaneous: $45

Sample Budget #2

Income: $1,200
Bills: $673
>   Rent (utilities, etc. included): $500
>   Credit Card: $100
>   Cable: $28
>   Phone: $32
>   Life Insurance: $13

Other Expenditures: $527
>   Food: $300
>   Transportation: $80
>   Entertainment: $100
>   Miscellaneous: $47

Sample Budget #3

Income: $3,500
Bills: $1,619
> Mortgage: $700
> Electric: $128
> Gas Heat: $73
> Water: $45
> Sewage: $32
> Cable: $58
> Garbage: $22
> Cell Phone, Internet, Cable Package Deal: $100
> Home Phone: $35
> Car Payment: $225
> Vehicle Insurance: $93
> Person 1 Life Insurance: $60
> Persons 2 Life Insurance: $32
> Person 3 Life Insurance: $8
> Persons 4 Life Insurance: $8

Other Expenditures: $1881
> Investments: $150
> Groceries: $800
> Takeout: $250
> Household Expenditures: $150
> Entertainment: $300
> Gas for Vehicles: $150
> Miscellaneous: $81

Food - $600 allotted

Date	Description	Amount	Remaining Balance
5-1	Pizza Place - 2 lg pizzas	$24.32	$575.68
5-3	Local Market - eggs, milk, bread, fruit	$17.25	$558.43
5-4	Deli - turkey, cheddar, roast beef, colby	$28.50	$529.93
5-6	Coffee Shop - bagel, muffin, 2 lattes	$12.29	$517.64
5-7	Farmer's Market - veggies	$32	$485.64
5-9	Bakery - Birthday Cake	$35	$450.64
5-9	Convenience Store - Ice cream	$10.60	$440.04
5-9	Vending Machine - peanuts, chips, candy	$3.75	$436.29
5-13	Grocery Store - buns, steaks, pasta, veggies	$88.79	$347.50
5-17	Deli - 3 sandwiches, salad, cheese, pickles	$40.28	$307.22

continued...

Sample Budget Page #2

Entertainment- $125 allotted

Date	Description	Amount	Remaining Balance
5-1	Movies	$20	$105
5-7	Local Petting Zoo	$27	$78
5-13	Museum	$18	$60
5-14	Movie Rental	$8.48	$51.52
5-20	Bowling	$32	$19.52
5-27	Mini Golf	$18	$1.52

Remaining Balance = $1.52

Bills

Amount allotted:_____$1100_____

Bill	Date Received	Date Due	Amount Allotted	Amount Due	Balance (+/-)
Mortgage	3rd	28	$550	$550	$0
Electric	2nd	21	$100	$94	+ $6
Gas	7th	23	$70	$70	$0
Water	12th	26	$35	$34.50	+ $.50
Sewage	5th	28	$32	$32	$0
Garbage	8th	24	$21	$20.95	+ $.05
Cable	13th	25	$58	$58	$0
Phone	15th	27	$65	$67.25	- $2.25
Internet	12th	27	$33	$32.95	+ $.05
Person 1 Life Insurance	11th	25	$10	$10	$0
Person 2 Life Insurance	11th	25	$45	$45	$0
Vehicle Insurance	12th	26	$81	$81	$0

Balance:_____ + $4.35_____

50

Bills

Amount allotted:_____$1,000_____

Bill	Amount Allotted	Amount Due	Balance (+/-)
Mortgage	$450	$450	$0
Electric	$100	$94	+ $6
Gas	$70	$70	$0
Water	$35	$34.50	+ $.50
Sewage	$32	$32	$0
Garbage	$21	$20.95	+ $.05
Cable	$58	$58	$0
Phone	$67	$67.23	- $0.23
Internet	$33	$32.95	+ $.05
Person 1 Life Insurance	$10	$10	$0
Person 2 Life Insurance	$45	$45	$0
Vehicle Insurance (yearly bill)	$81 to alternate savings	$81 monthly cost ($972/year)	$0

Balance:_____+ $2.33_____

51

Blank Budget Pages

You can create your own budget pages, or you can copy the following examples to use for your budget.

Blank Budget #1

Income:
Bills:
      Rent (utilities, etc. included):
      Credit Card:
      Cable: $
      Phone:
      Life Insurance:
Other Expenditures:
      Food:
      Transportation:
      Entertainment:
      Miscellaneous:

Blank Budget #2

Income:
Bills:

        Mortgage:
        Electric:
        Gas Heat:
        Water:
        Sewage:
        Cable:
        Garbage:
        Cell Phone:
        Internet:
        Cable/Satellite:
        Home Phone:
        Car Payment:
        Vehicle Insurance:
        Person 1 Life Insurance:
        Persons 2 Life Insurance:
        Person 3 Life Insurance:
        Persons 4 Life Insurance:

Other Expenditures:
        Investments:
        Groceries:
        Takeout:
        Household Items:
        Entertainment:
        Gas for Vehicles:
        Miscellaneous:

Blank Budget #3

Income: $_____
Bills:

————
————
————
————
————
————
————
————
————
————
————
————
————

Other Expenditures:

————
————
————
————
————
————
————
————
————

Blank Budget Category Page

Category:_____ **Amount allotted:**_____

Date	Description	Amount	Balance

Remaining Balance:_____

Bills
Amount allotted:_____

Bill	Date Due	Amount

Bills

Amount allotted:_____

Bill	Date Received	Date Due	Amount Allotted	Amount Due	Balance

Balance:_____

Additional Resources

I do not endorse any resource listed. They are listed as possible sources for more information about budgeting. I can't guarantee their accuracy. There are numerous more resources available besides the ones listed. Feel free to find your own.

Websites:

www.free-financial-advice.net/create-budget.html

www.seekingsuccess.com/articles/art138.php

www.foxway.com

www.microsheet.com/budget_sheets.htm

www.betterbudgeting.com/budgetformsfree.htm

www.householdbudgetnerd.com

www.kiplinger.com/tools/budget

www.money.cnn.com/magazines/moneymag/money101/lesson2/

Books:

Quick and Easy Budget Book: A Practical Workbook for Balancing Your Household Budget by Dianna Barra

BudgetYes! 21st Century Solutions for Taking Control of Your Money Now! by John L. Macko and Jane E. Chidester

The Budget Kit: The Common Cents Money Management Workbook by Judy Lawrence

How To Setup A Family Budget Even If You Never Have Before by Dannie Elwins

Family Budget ... Demystified! by Paul Jackson

The Bible (New Living Translation) Matthew 25:29

How To Setup A Family Budget by Fiona Halle

A Mom's Guide to Family Finances by Ellie Kay

FAQ's

Below is a list of frequently asked questions. You may have already read some of this information in previous chapters, but the following questions and answers may clarify it for you.

1. Isn't a budget restrictive?

Making a budget is setting boundaries on your spending, so although that may seem restrictive at first, it can actually be quite freeing following a budget and not having to worry about whether or not you'll have enough money to pay your end-of-the-month bills.

However, budgets are only as restrictive as you make them. If you allot $100 a month for movie rentals, you can spend $100 a month on movie rentals. If you only allot $10 per month for movie rentals, but you normally spend $20, then it will be restrictive. Start slow. Don't try to make huge spending cuts right away. Remember, you don't have to make spending cuts at all. It's entirely up to you.

2. What if my income changes?

If you get a raise, or if your income decreases, you can calculate your new actual income and adjust your budget accordingly.

3. Why do I need a budget?

You need a budget in order to be in control of your finances, to see where your money is going, and to make sure you'll be able to pay all of your bills.

A budget will also be able to help you determine what you can and can't afford - a good thing to know before deciding on a new car, a bigger house, or even weekly takeout.

If you want to build up your savings account, a budget is practically a necessity. It can help you trim your expenses, freeing up more money for savings.

4. You mentioned the word "tithe". What is tithing?

A tithe is a voluntary offering of 10% of your income to God, usually contributed to your church in support of its services. It's a biblical principle with references in the books of Genesis, Hebrews, Numbers, Deuteronomy, 2 Chronicles, Amos, Malachi, and 1 Corinthians.

5. What if I overspend?

If you overspend, you may need to adjust the amount of money allotted to your budget categories. You can continue adjusting your budget as needed.

However, if you're spending more than you earn, you'll need to exercise more self control with regard to your purchases, or you could consider finding a second source of income.

6. What if I don't spend all of the money I allotted?

If you don't spend all of the money you allotted, pat yourself on the back, you've come in under budget!

Seriously though, under is better than over. You could put the extra money in a savings account or pay extra on your mortgage, but it's your money, so you can spend it or save it as you see fit.

7. What if I just can't get my budget to work?

If you can't get your budget to work for you, don't give up. You may need some professional assistance. You may want to consult a financial planner or other qualified financial advisor.

~~~*Notes*~~~

~~~_Notes_~~~

About The Author

Randi Lynn Millward resides in Marienville, Pennsylvania, with her husband and their three children. Randi is currently a full-time mom and a part-time author and columnist.

In 2004, Randi received a certificate in Creative Writing and Manuscript Marketing from Charter Oak State College of West Redding, Connecticut. In 2006, she received her ASB in Business Management with an option in Human Resources Management from Penn Foster College of Scranton, Pennsylvania.

In addition to this book, Randi is the author of *100 Income Streams for Full-time Moms: Because Your Children are Your Full-time Job*, *Beyond the Traditional Lemonade Stand: Creative Business Stand Plans for Children of All Ages,* and *50 Eggcellent Egg-Free Breakfast Recipes: Because People with Egg Allergies Deserve a Good Breakfast, Too!*. Randi also writes a weekly financial column for SingleMom.com, and her writing has appeared in the Business Builders section of the Christian Work At Home Moms (CWAHM) newsletter on more than a dozen occasions.

To contact Randi or order additional copies of this book, or any other book that she's authored, visit her website at:

www.RandiLynnMillward.com

www.RandiLynnMillward.com

www.ingramcontent.com/pod-product-compliance
Lightning Source LLC
Chambersburg PA
CBHW060709030426
42337CB00017B/2825